New Tales from Aesop

New Tales

from Aesop

(for reading aloud)

by Paul Roche

Illustrations by Pandora Smith

Notre Dame/University of Notre Dame Press
London/Honeyglen Publishing Limited

Copyright © 1982 by
University of Notre Dame Press
Notre Dame, Indiana 46556

First published in the United Kingdom in 1982 by
Honeyglen Publishing Limited
Duchess of Bedford House
16 Duchess of Bedford Walk
London, W8 7QL England

Library of Congress Cataloging in Publication Data

Roche, Paul, 1927-
    New tales from Aesop (for reading aloud)
    Summary: Presents 80 of Aesop's classic tales
rewritten for reading aloud.
    [1. Fables]   I. Aesop.   II. Title.
PR6068.026N4   821'.914   81-40447
ISBN 0-268-00597-4   AACR2

Manufactured in the United States of America

For my two sons—
  Tobit and Martin

The author wishes to express his gratitude
to the Edwig Vogelstein Foundation,
which made possible the completion of this book.

Preface

The fable, whether in prose or verse, is a capsule of wisdom dispensed through parable. It takes delight in the way people, animals and things masquerade in their individuality and thereby make us wisely smile at our own. We enjoy recognising ourselves in our cruder virtues and simpler vices, provided it be in disguise: the satiric disguise of a hoodwinking fox or an ambitious bullfrog. Handed down orally, the fable set out to be succinctly memorable. After generations of repetition and embellishment, it became hard and smooth—as incisive as the cut marble on which were inscribed the winners at the Olympic Games.

After the poets had got hold of it, this lapidary concision grew into a literary genre in its own right and aimed at being something more than an expanded proverb: a mere residuum of garnered wisdom. The fable set out unequivocally to be an object of art, a monument in miniature. And yet as a literary form it continued the illusion of being elementary, even primitive. When one comes to a work like the Metamorphoses of Ovid, the paradox is complete. Here, stories of the gods and goddesses of the utmost naivety are told in a language of such finesse that the sophisticated reader derives his pleasure precisely from the contrast.

And so, from the Greek and Latin versions of Aesop to the parables of the Panchatantra, the fable remained a childlike thing though never fashioned for children. What is surprising is that though it soon outdistanced simple delight in plot and story, the fable seems to have been the stock property of nursery and school through the ages. And the trend is with us still. In the interests of instruction and instant comprehension the subtleties held in solution by poetry are precipitated out and the results siphoned off as mere animal tales. In such macerations, love of anecdote is substituted for the magic of parable and the characters become no longer symbols, or even sublimations of the human, but naturalistically anthromorphic.

Yet the Aesopian fable at its best takes no account of age and cannot be exploited for mere information. Like poetry, it is illuminative rather than didactic—even when being didactic—and like such masterpieces as Alice in Wonderland, Hans Andersen and the Nursery Rhymes it enters the bloodstream before and beyond the acquisition of knowledge. It gives something to all, and it gives it immediately, but holds in reserve a still luminous treasure.

In my own retellings, I have been faithful to Aesop's basic themes and plots (surprisingly bald and uninteresting in the "original" Greek), but have followed my fancy in the manner of unfolding them. With La Fontaine temptingly and dangerously in mind I have purposely not re-read him; for when it comes to vividness, wit, the unforgettable vignette and sheer delight in animal-cum-human shrewdness, La Fontaine is the master, and I should have found myself trying to imitate his instances rather than follow his inspiration.

In the matter of style, I decided on an idiom which though contemporary was not without literary echoes: cadences from a past when a certain formality was the soul of both simplicity and elegance. This allowed me a wide and motile vocabulary and the opportunity of directness as well as of the rounded gesture. It also encouraged me to be adventuresome and to take risks with every kind of prosodic device. There is rhyme and no rhyme, half-rhyme and cross-rhyme. There are lines ending only in assonance, and only in consonance. There is metre and stress-rhythm, blank verse and the "freewheeling iambic." Occasionally there is straight prose. The only thing there is not is "syllabics," a count of syllables regardless of accent or rhythm. The reader is not asked to be conscious of such things—in fact I should be alarmed if he noticed them at all—but I hope that the poetically curious will be enter-

8

tained by this variety. If I express a wish that the tales be read aloud, it is only because I have designed them expressly for the ear.

One last and perhaps too obvious point: where inventiveness and humour have been the hallmarks of a long and cumulative tradition, there is no version of Aesop which may certainly claim to be *the* original, and no retelling which is not in its own way *an* original.

P.R.

ΒΟΤΡΥΣ ΜΕΛΑΙΝΗΣ ΑΜΠΕΛΟΥ ΠΑΡΩΕΙΗ
ΑΠΕΚΡΕΜΑΝΤΟ ΤΟΥΣ ΔΕ ΠΟΙΚΙΛΗ ΠΛΗΡΕΙΣ
ΙΔΟΥΣΑ ΚΕΡΔΩ ΠΟΛΛΑΚΙΣ ΜΕΝ ΩΡΜΗΘΗ
ΠΗΔΩΣ ΑΠΟΣΣΙΝ ΠΟΡΟΥΡΗΣ ΘΙΓΕΙΝ ΩΡΗΣ
ΗΝ ΓΑΡ ΠΕΠΕΙΡΟΣ ΚΕΙΣ ΤΡΥΓΗΤΟΝ ΑΚΜΑΙΗ
ΚΑΜΝΟΥΣΑ ΔΑΛΛΩΣ ΟΥ ΓΑΡΙΣ ΧΥΕ ΨΑΥΕΙΝ
ΠΑΡΗΛΘΕΝ ΟΥΤΩ ΒΟΥΚΟΛΟΥΣΑ ΤΗΝ ΛΥΠΕΙΝ
ΟΜΘΑΞΟ ΒΟΤΡΥΣ ΟΥΠΕΠΕΙΡΟΣ ΩΣ ΩΜΗΝ

The Fox and The Grapes
as told by Valerius Babrius

History of the Fable

The Beast-tale is such a simple thing that we do not need to be told that ever since mankind first hunted the stag or tamed the wild ass, his proximity to animals led him to introduce them into folklore. The fable proper is also a simple thing, but in it the animals are made to go a step further and not only to act with human motives and feelings but point with a claw or a paw or a hoof at man's own nature and draw a moral.

It is not surprising that the ancestry of a form so elementary should be lost in civilizations earlier than the Greek. Its evolution can be traced back both in India, probably to sources emanating from Buddha himself in the sixth century B.C., and in Asia Minor (in records of clay tablets inscribed with cuneiform writing): back to ancient Babylon. It was the Greeks, however, who gave the fable its classic shape: the directness, brevity, epigram and humour we expect of it. And though there are no fables in Homer, the process is evident not long after him in such poets as Hesiod and Archilochus: two hundred years at least before the assumed birth of Aesop. It was Aesop nevertheless, in so far as we can depend on the scanty records of the man himself, who established the fable as a form. We do not know how many he himself invented, or what was the political motivation behind many of them, but by the end of the fifth century B.C. the fables of the Aesopian repetoire were everywhere, from the mainland of Greece to the banks of the Nile. What is more, whether they were used in public speeches, quoted in after-dinner tabletalk or exploited by pedagogues, so thorough was Aesop's stamp on this particular tradition that from then onwards all fables were ascribed to him as a matter of course, even those current before his time and those going into circulation after he was dead. The canon finally comprised a corpus of more than seven hundred fables.

Little is known of the man himself, though a copious legend exists and a unique "Life" dating from about the first century of our era, which is fascinating but obviously apocryphal. Most of what we know with any reliability comes from Herodotus, writing in the latter half of the fifth century B.C. From him we learn that Aesop existed in the sixth century, was associated with the island of Samos off the coast of Asia Minor, may have been the slave of a Samian citizen called Iadmon, composed stories, and was murdered by the people of Delphi. From other sources we gather that he was either a Thracian or a Phrygian*, and that he offended the Delphians, who "planted" a chalice from the temple in his baggage and then hurled him to his death on the charge of sacrilege.

As to the person of Aesop, legend has it that he was small and ugly: a potbellied, squash-nosed hunchback, who was also crosseyed, bandy-legged and a stammerer: in fact a freak, but a freak whose genius shone against the foil of his grotesque appearance. The ingenuity, wisdom and wit, the invention and sparkle of his words, were the jewels in this toad's head. He was courted by the great. People flocked to hear him.

One naturally asks: do we actually have Aesop's versions of his fables? The answer unfortunately is, certainly not. Even if his fables were written down by him (which does not seem likely) or by his contemporaries, the versions that have reached us have such a complicated history that there is no way of knowing how near any of them is to Aesop's own way of telling them. One can only suppose, given Aesop's fame as a raconteur, that when these versions come to life with point and directness, they are nearest to Aesop in spirit, but that when they are lifeless (as the extant Greek prose versions are), or overloaded and meretricious (as many have been), they are not.

*The Thracians were from northern Greece. They supposedly colonised Bryges in Asia Minor, which came to be called Phrygia.

12

What in fact do we possess? First of all, there are fragments of a papyrus scroll dating from the first century A.D. and containing fables in Greek prose. This may well be the elusive collection known to have been made by Demetrius of Phaleron at Athens about 300 B.C. but since lost. The papyrus is too fragmentary to be of use.

Next we have a few fables narrated by Greek and Latin authors of the second and first centuries. The Fox in the Oak Tree, for instance, the Town Mouse and the Country Mouse, and the Ox and the Bullfrog, are all told by Horace besides being found in later versions. In this group one must also place the various Greek authors—notably Plutarch—of the first and second centuries who use fables in the body of their work.

Third on our list, and the earliest extant collection, are the renderings of Phaedrus, a Greek freedman of Augustus, done by him into Latin iambic verse during the first century A.D. These have a simplicity and charm of their own, not unmixed with a certain satiric piquancy: an element that was to grow through the ages as the Aesopic fable permeated Europe—to reach its most perfect expression in the seventeenth century with the fables of La Fontaine.

Fourthly, but the first extant collection in Greek of known authorship, are the iambic renditions of Valerius Babrius, a hellenized Roman and tutor to the young son of the Emperor Alexander Sevérus. Babrius, who wrote not later than the end of the second century, may well have used as his source a corpus of ancient fable based both on the collection of Demetrius and on the "Libyan" fables whose provenance, through Ceylon, was India. His versions are altogether more imaginative than the earlier Latin iambic compositions of Phaedrus; they show charm and skill though they reflect the literary selfconsciousness of his age. We have only two of his ten books.

Fifth on the list is another Latin one, that of Avianus the Roman who, using Babrius rather than Phaedrus as his source, turned forty-two fables into elegiac verse about 400 A.D. The results are somewhat involuted and padded but they seem to have enjoyed a long popularity. It was this version together with Phaedrus' which, in a series of prose paraphrases dating from the fifth century onwards, may have been the chief bridge that connected the lost fables of antiquity, through the middle-ages to modern times.*

Sixthly and lastly (and probably most controversially) there are over forty manuscripts of anonymous versions in Greek prose. The question remains: where do these come from? Until yesterday some scholars believed that the vast bulk of these Greek prose versions were written at a very late date: not before the ninth century. Joseph Jacobs, for instance, writing towards the turn of the century, considered them no more than late prose paraphrasings of Babrius, and not very good at that. Experts today are more inclined to believe that the earliest of these Greek prose renderings—though their manuscripts date from only the tenth to the sixteenth centuries—are based on a nucleus of versions that go back to the end of the second century A.D. at least. Some say further: into pre-Christian times. Be that as it may, the style of these 350 or so stories contained in the prose collections varies, from a classical simplicity and naturalness to a bald and sometimes infantile flatness.

Finally, what of the morals attached to the beginnings or ends of the fables in the way we have come to expect: when did this habit begin? Again, there is no certainty. Although most of the fables in the extant collections have morals tacked on to them, it seems improbable that this was always so. Phaedrus put his at the beginning: a tradition I have returned to. In any case, one is inclined to agree with Dr. Lloyd Daly in the Introduction to his most useful collection,* that the morals are little more than an insult to our intelligence. There seems to be no appealing way of attaching morals to the ends of stories unless one turns them into embellishments, as La Fontaine did, and makes them into ironic homilies in their own right—full of acumen and charm.

---

*That is, if we include the early fourteenth century collection made from various sources by Maximus Planudes, a Byzantine scholar, which lasted in popularity till the publication of the Augustana collection in 1812.

*_Aesop without Morals_, by Lloyd W. Daly, Thomas Yoseloff, 1961.

The Fables

(In alphabetical order)

15

16

THE FOX, THE COCK AND THE DOG

(Cunning is often caught in its own coils)

A hungry Fox unable to believe his eyes,
Saw one night etched against the stars
A magnificent Cock—almost within his reach.
"Wake up, fine bird!" he called, "the world is rich:
I have such news for you it cannot wait."
The Cock, high up, blinked and answered, "What?"
"Ah," said the Fox, his mouth already wet,
"King Lion has made a universal truce:
No beast may hurt a bird at any price.
From this time on we all shall live at peace."
"Remarkable!" the Cock replied. "You mean
That *I'll* be safe from you, and you from men?"
"Exactly that. Come, take my paw, come down.
Let all the past be healed in one embrace."
"Wait," said Cock craning his neck, "I see
Someone who'll want to join our jubilee.
Yes look, he leaps towards us eagerly."
"Hm!" said Fox. "Can you tell me who?"
"Only the farmer's Dog. I think you know
Him. . . . Yes? . . . Ah, must you really go?
I thought the three of us were all about to kiss."
And he added just as Fox displayed his back:
"Surely you and he would love to speak
Of brotherly love and universal peace?"
"Be glad to, yes—but have no guarantee,"
(Shouted the Fox already far away)
"That Master Dog has heard King Lion's decree."

THE LION AND THE MOUSE

(The small can sometimes aid the great)

A Lion once dreamed a vivid dream:
He thought a mouse had run across his nose;
And shaking wide awake with a mighty sneeze
Found a mouse actually in his paws.
The thing was pitifully slight and small,
Quite useless throught the Lion for a meal.
It held its little squirrel hands out praying
And trembled like a piece of fluff vibrating.
"I pardon you," the Lion thundered. "Scatter!
Off with you. You're not for my cuisine.
Noblesse oblige. I could not be so mean.
You would not even make hors d'oeuvres for supper."

The Mouse's heart though small went pitter-patter.
He shone his thanks from polished beady eyes.
"O Life, my lady and my little ones," he cried,
"What *would* become of you if I
Were lionised to line a lion's inside
Or marinated for a lion's dinner? ... "
"Sire," he said, "a day may come when in a crise
this my trespass on your nose
May bring you help from this unworthy mouse."

The Lion laughed and let the pigmy go.
But as it happened, not long afterwards,
He fell into a netted hooded hole,
Thrashed and tore the loops to no avail,
Found himself enmeshed beyond all hope
And waited for the dreaded break of dawn.

Then at midnight, softly trickling down,
He felt a mouse come whispering on the ropes,
Stop at the knots and start to nibble through.
And long before the fatal dawn, the truth
Broke on him: that he was being unbound—
The Mouse that he had saved had come to save.
It was the little come to aid the great,
The Mouse that *he* had laughed at and forgave.

THE RABBITS AND THE FROGS

(There is always someone worse off than you are)

It seemed to the Rabbits that as a race they had reached warren-bottom. Everybody preyed upon them: not only the foxes, the weasels, the wolves, but even man. He made pies of their flesh and coats of their skins. And, as if that were not enough, hawks swooped by day and owls by night. No wonder the Rabbits developed a nervous twitch and lived from second to second.

One day wild horses stampeded through the meadows, filling the air with their neighing. They made the hill rock with the beat of their hooves. The Rabbits fled en masse to a nearby lake, their elders crying out as they ran:

"It's no use trying to live, Children. Let us plunge into the waters of this lake and drown ourselves."

But as the Rabbits approached the shores of the lake, they frightened hundreds of frogs and heard and saw them fling themselves into the water. Then the chief Rabbit called out:

"Stop, Children, stop. Let us live. Things are not as bad as they seem. These Frogs have just proved to us that there are others worse off than we are."

THE BOY WHO CRIED "WOLF!"

(A liar is not believed even when he tells the truth)

Momus, bright from his birth but a callous lad,
Began to develop a curious sense of fun.
Grazing his father's sheep one afternoon
(A stonesthrow from the village in the sun)
He stared at the nibbling animals and said:
"What a sheepish bunch! What googley eyes!
How vacuous! And lips how prim and thin!
Sillier than chickens, I declare."
Then, smacking his thighs, with a devilish grin:
"Wolf! Wolf! Help! Help!" he cries,
With voice to rend the air and raise the dead.
As the wretched siesta-ridden men,
Women and children of the village ran
From their beds in every shape and size
(half-dressed, undressed, dragging tunics on),
Momus shouted louder: "Awake, arise . . .
Wolf! Wolf! Faster! Faster!"
Then rolled upon the grass with laughter.

Reckless of the havoc of his jest,
This same youth hardly two weeks after—
Bored again with flock and fold and pasture—
(In the morning this time) raised his shout
"Wolf! Wolf!", repeating the disaster.
And as the villagers came tumbling out,
"Ha ha ha!" he mocked, "I like the old jokes best."
The third time he called, response was none.
This time at dusk Momus roared
"Wolf! Wolf! Wake up!" with real conviction.
No one stirred though Momus roared till he was dumb.
And this time real wolves had come.

22

THE CAT AND APHRODITE

(Nature will out)

This event is rare,
   probably unique:
A Cat once fell in love with a fine young man,
   comely of face and of godlike physique;
And being eaten up with frustration—
   seeing no way to bring to consummation
   an affair with a human—
She went to Aphrodite, pierced with love's pang.

The goddess,
   who had a weakness
   for the whole feline race
   especially cats,
And was nowise indisposed to amorous acrobats,
   gave her a new body and a new face;
In fact changed her into a girl so irresistible
   that the young man fell
   deeply in love at sight;
   and in no time at all
Had wed her, taken her home, and was celebrating the nuptial night.

All of which Aphrodite was not slow to bless.
But when the young couple were lying at ease in bed
   (enjoying a short respite)
The goddess,
   smiling down from Olympus,
   said to herself, she said:
"I wonder if that girl is still a cat at heart?
One cannot guess
   the limits of alchemy or art.
I'd give anything to know.
Can anyone really escape
   change of instinct with a change of shape?"

And so,
 gratifying an immediate whim,
 she let loose a mouse
 right under the bride's nose:
 had it actually scudding over the bridal sheets.
Whereat, the girl leapt from the bedclothes,
 tore herself from the arms of her groom,
 and quite regardless of him
 or his incredulous shrieks,
Went running and pouncing round the room.

"Ah!" sighed Aphrodite from above,
 "there is no doubt
 that nature will out—
Even in love."

THE WOLF AND THE LAMB

(For the wicked: Might is right)

Lamb's ears felt assaulted. The rough voice was utterly unlike his mother's.

"How dare you, sir?" it growled. "How dare you?"

He lifted his woolly head and trembled. A little distance upstream from where he was drinking, a large grizzled animal glared at him with hot-looking eyes. Could this be a wolf? His teeth were gleaming.

"I am speaking to you, sir," rasped the voice again. "How dare you muddle the crystal of my stream? Impertinent ovine!"

"Oh no, sir, I cannot be doing that," Lamb replied, standing where he was: "I barely lick the top of the water, and the stream comes from you to me."

"What! You call me a liar?"

The Wolf took three steps nearer. His look was paralyzing. "Ah, now I see. You're the one who spread all those lies about me last year."

"How could I, sir? I was only born this spring." Lamb's voice came high and tremulous.

"Smart, eh? ... Always an answer? Well, if it wasn't you it was your brother."

"I have no brother," Lamb said. "I am an only lamb."

"Then it was your cousin. What care I? You're all the same: you and your shepherds and dogs. You hound me from my woods and fields."

"Me, sir? Oh no."

Lamb was on the point of tears; he wanted to run to his mother. But the Wolf had moved to within four paces, and he could smell the beast's rancid breath.

"Yes, you do. You start young. But I'm going to make an example of you."

"I'm not to blame, sir," Lamb bleated, "really, I'm not. And if your Lordship ..."

26

But Lamb did not finish his sentence. In one spring the Wolf crumpled him to the ground.

"I mean to eat you," he said, in a snarl that crawled from his throat.

And he did.

THE STAG AND THE FAWN

(A born coward will remain one)

A brave-looking Stag with antlers strong and branched
Was approached by his son one day, a Fawn, who asked:
"Father, nature has made you bigger than dogs,
Faster too, and should you fail to dodge
The hounds, she's given you your glorious horns
To run them through and scatter them in hordes.
Why then do you flee from them in fear?"
The Stag with a cough and shy of looking fierce,
Said, "Son—ahem—what you say is true,
I'm fast and strong, and yet to tell the truth,
The moment I scent the pack and hear them bay,
Something deep inside me makes me run away."

THE FOX AND THE GOAT

(Look before you leap)

The Fox waited:
He had fallen into a well
And had been trying to get out half the day.
Its sides were too steep, too deep,
Though he had jumped till his strength was wasted.
He gazed up hopelessly at the sheer wall.
It happened that a Goat passed that way
And putting his head over the top
Asked curiously what the Fox was doing there.
"Enjoying myself. They say
There's going to be a mighty drought,
So I'm down here drinking my fill.
Why don't you come down yourself and share?"
So Goat let himself down into the well;
Applied himself to the water as Fox with a shout
Mounted his back and using his head as a sill
Sprang into freedom, then from the edge of the well
Called down to the flabbergasted Goat:
"It's all yours, friend, have a good swill.
But in future I advise you to take note:
When people enthusiastically press you to share,
Beware."

THE BULLFROG AND THE BULL

(Self-conceit can lead to self-destruction)

"Father," a goggle-eyed junior Bullfrog croaked
From among the marshes where a bigger Bullfrog soaked:
"I've seen the hugest, most enormous thing
Standing in the meadows with brackets on its head,
A tail like a tassle and through its nose a ring.
Is it a rhinoceros or a giant toad?"
"Tut tut, my son!" the senior Bullfrog said:
"It's only a Bull, and as to its giant size
I think your calf-frog fancy's overflowed.
It's taller than me perhaps, but as to spread,
Great Bullrush no! I more than equalize."
Saying which, this Bullfrog breathed and blew
His carcass up: outwards from within.
"Why, I'll make myself as big as two."
"Perhaps, but still, compared to him you're thin,"
The small frog said and watched him as he grew.
"As big as this?" "Oh, bigger, bigger." "Wait."
He drew a breath that forced him to inflate
To such a size his skin was a balloon.
"Not as big as—?" Bang! He spoke too soon . . .
They never found the places he was strewn.

THE HARE AT THE MEETING

(A line of action needs the means to enforce it)

"Fair shares for all," said the Hare
At a meeting of lion and bear,
   But without claws
   And nothing but paws
He never got further than there.

ZEUS AND THE TORTOISE

(There is no place like home)

It was Zeus's wedding,
   with every animal invited,
   in fact expected to be there
   just at his bidding.
But after his and Juno's vows were plighted
   the king of gods became aware
   that the only creature still not there
   was the Tortoise.
   So he said to Juno: "I wonder why?
Does the lowly Tortoise mean to thwart us?"
And Juno answered in that slightly acid
   way of hers: "Ask him yourself. Have him brought here.
   You mustn't let him be so placid."
Then she went on:
   "If the Tortoise is too haughty to comply
   he must learn a lesson,
   let him be taught here."

30

So the Tortoise hobbled in
    and was arraigned before the seat of Zeus.
His words were spare, hardly one might say, profuse;
    if anything a bit obtuse.
"Sire," he said, "there is no place like home.
    That's my excuse."
He was so obviously sincere
    that Zeus
    nonplussed
    found anger, sarcasm and disgust
    melting before the wish to benefact.
So he said: "I trust
    one cannot teach a tortoise tact . . .
    There's no place like home, eh?"
"Sire, you cannot doubt it."
"Very well: henceforth I say
    you shall never be without it.
    Wherever you may roam
    you shall carry round your own most private home."

THE FLY AND THE BROTH

(What cannot be avoided can still be accepted
with courage and grace)

When a Fly fell into the brink
Of some Broth and started to sink
    She said: "I have dined
    And am very well wined,
I am ready for heaven, I think."

THE GOOSE THAT LAID THE GOLDEN EGGS

(Greed destroys the source of good)

The phenomenon
   had been going on
   for several weeks.
Yes, the Goose actually laid golden eggs:
   huge nuggets smooth as wax
   and heavy as lead.
The Man and his Wife went down on their knees
   and thanked Hermes
   for having so rewarded their years
   of poverty and piety . . .
"But we could do with a bigger house,"
   said the wife. "Of course,"
   the Man replied.
And after a few days
   and a few more golden eggs,
   they both said:
"Why not servants and a carriage? . . .
Then there's that dowry for our beloved daughter's marriage."
Soon the golden eggs could hardly keep pace
   with the couple's galloping desires.
They became rapacious
   and they gave themselves airs.
"We must have money," was the Wife's cry.
"Put pepper in the Goose's mash:
   perhaps
   it will then lay two eggs at a time . . .
   I need a new costume."
Then one day the Wife
   nudged her man with a terrible gleam in her eye.
"Cut it open," she said, cold:
   "it's an enormous bird
   and full of gold."

32

"I can't," he said.
So she put in his hands a knife.
"Go on," she said:
    "I owe the dressmaker, the hairdresser, the grocer,
    the chemist, the wine shop, the jeweller . . .
    we simply must have money—
    or do you want me to borrow?"
"All right," he said, "but it's damnable."
So he laid the Goose on the kitchen table,
    stunned it and opened it up.
Then he gave a great booming laugh, dismally unfunny.
"My dear, you'll never guess,"
    he said; and his tears of rage, frustration and sorrow
    broke in a flood.
"There's nothing inside the Goose
    but ordinary flesh and blood."

THE OLD MAN AND DEATH

(We do not always mean what we say)

An old woodcutter, bent with the years and saddled with regrets, was shouldering a bundle of sticks he had cut when, overcome with hopelessness, he tossed it to the ground and blurted out:

"What's the good of living for one such as I? Alone, neglected, full of aches and pains. . . . O Death, I wish you would come and take me."

"At your service, Old Man," said Death suddenly appearing—famished and grisly. "I heard you call me. What was it you said you wanted?"

The Old Man gulped, stepping back from the skeleton presence.

"Please help me to pick up that bundle of sticks, sir," he said.

THE MAN, THE LION AND THE STATUE

(Valid argument must be objective)

A Man
Was having an argument
With a somewhat intelligent
Lion.
"There is no question," said the Man
(And his manner was militant),
"But that men are stronger than lions:
They have more brains.
Come with me now
And I'll show you this is so."
He walked the Lion to the public park,
Pointed to a Statue and said: "Look,
Isn't it obvious?"
The Lion looked at the Statue,
Which was of Hercules
Overcoming a lion and tearing his
Mouth in two;
Then he made this commentary:
"The only obvious thing to me
Is that a *man* put up this effigy."

THE FROGS WHO DESIRED A KING

(Let well enough alone)

The Frogs lived happily as anarchists.
All day they played in their watery marsh,
Come rain, come sun, come mists,
Tumbling and plopping into the mush
Or sitting sodden in the wet.
Then some smart ones of the younger set,
The intelligentsia of the bogs,
Carried this resolution in their parliament:
    "Frogdom is world-weary of democracy.
    Its usefulness is finished.
    Let us ask Zeus for a monarchy.
    For, the silliness of frogs
    Has increased, is increasing
    And ought to be diminished."

They sent contingents croaking by the dozen
To the throne of Zeus to importune
The Father-of-the-gods to send a sovereign.
Then during his siesta one afternoon
When he had been disturbed for the sixteenth time,
The Thunder-bolter reaching out an arm
Tossed a log down from Olympus—Kerplash!
It landed in the marsh with an immense splash.
"There's your king," he said with a dismissive yawn.
"Do him homage and obey . . . Now go away."

It was the great event of the afternoon:
Frogs leapt, dived, swam in disarray.
Some hid themsleves under a leaf,
While the log lay there without a sign of life.

And presently one frog and then another
Swivelled an oblique eye with hesitant croaks
And whispered: "O sister, O my brother,
        What stolid majesty!
        What royal gravity!
        The real thing—a king."

One by one the Frogs came out to see.
In all directions frogs bobbed up like corks
And soon were thick as ants about the throne.
It then appeared to members intellectual
That the monarch was extremely dull
If not downright ineffectual.
One of them, a stripling, made so bold
As to clamber on the royal back and get a hold,
And seeing this impertinence
Was suffered with indifference,
Proceeded to shout and sing along the length of him,
Till even the hoi polloi grasped the hoax
And deafened the Almighty with their croaks.
        "Our prince is an invertebrate.
        He is not even animate.
        Send us a real 'Turannos'
        Long to reign over us."

Zeus almost snatched a lightning fork;
Instead despatched a dictatorial stork
Who stood in water morn till night
And gobbled frogs up regally
With voracious appetite.
"That's not the kind of king we want, sire,"
A desperate delegation pleaded finally.
        "Kings seldom are,"
Drawled the deity.

THE SOLDIER AND HIS HORSE

(Exploitation brings its own disaster)

Proud of his horse the Soldier fed
Him oats and barley through the war:
"My friend, you share my risks," he said,
"And you're the finest stallion here."
But when the war was over and done
And the panoplies of battle gone,
He turned him into beast of burden,
Worked him like a slave all day
    And gave him hay.
After a year, again there's war.
The Soldier and the stallion each
Shine and jingle as before.
Then said the poor exhausted Horse
Stumbling along beneath his weight:
"You'd better join the infantry, sir.
For though I'm decked out gay bedight
I'm not your stallion any more:
I'm broken, jaded, starved and worse—
You've gone and got yourself an ass.
And far from carrying *you* to war,
    I need a hearse."

THE FROGS AT THE SUN'S WEDDING

(Public celebrations can be shallow)

Every animal was there, the Sun
Was wed with music, feasting, dance and song:
Nuptials being since the birth of time
The best respite that Earth has from travail.
Among those wassailing were certain frogs,
And of their number one who spoke but little,
Ate even less, and did not drink at all.
Nor did he dance, but cast from time to time
Lugubrious eyes toward the bridegroom Sun.
A fellow frog then asked him why he gazed
With such a forlorn glance. The old Frog waved
His hands towards the wedding guests and said:
"Little know you what you celebrate."
When pressed for more, the savant Frog explained:
"Understand the function of the Sun.
He scorches frog spawn, addles eggs, he dries
Rivers up, and empties marshes, ponds.
If this is what a single sun can do,
What place will there be left to wallow in
Except the river Styx when he has young."

THE MOLE WHO LIED

(One excessive claim gives the lie to all)

A Mole whose brain was weak but active
Sought to make himself attractive.
He told his mother he could see—
Something that no mole can do.
"Oh yes," he said, "I see a tree,
I see some horses, I see you."
His mother on a sudden whim
Pushed beneath his sniffling nose
A wild but sweetly smelling rose.
"What's that?" she tartly asked of him.
"Why—er—Mum, that's a pebble."
"My son, save yourself the trouble.
You'll have to think of better lies
If you're so anxious to excel.
Not only have you useless eyes,
You've got a futile nose as well."

THE MAN AND THE SATYR

(The simple cannot distinguish)

A Man once wandered through a wood
And in the depths of it mistook
    His path and there was lost.
The time was winter, and the night
Falling on the falling whiteness
    Filled his gaze with fog.

40

Then groping through the brush, he saw
A lightly goatlike stepping form:
    A Satyr of the forest.
Who peered and pranced and then declared:
"Sir, my grotto's in the dell.
    Stay till morning there."

The Satyr led him through the trees
And staring backward was intrigued
    To see him blow his fingers.
"I blow on them to keep them warm,"
The Man explained. And thus they walked
    To the grotto in the dell.

He gave the man a smoking bowl
Of broth. The Man began to blow
    Upon the dish he held.
"And what's that for?" the Satyr asked.
"To cool the brew and cool it fast."
    Then Satyr with a yell

Leapt from his stool, his eyes ablaze:
"Out with you. Away! Away!
    I'll not have any part
With one whose mouth breathes hot and cold,
Like snow on fire and fire on snow.
    O Man, I say: depart."

THE TWO COCKS

(The proud shall be humbled and the humble exalted)

Two Cocks born from the same clutch,
Inevitably coming of age at the same time,
Found that more and more they must compete
For kingship of the same disputed patch,
The same roosts, and especially the esteem
Of the hens and pullets of the same hareem.
They came of age perforce and had to meet
Head on and spur to spur with bristling ruff.
They fought a drawn-out fierce and bloody match.
Feathers and beaks flew, talons slashed,
Until one Cock proclaimed he'd had enough
And ran discomfited inside a hutch
To brood on love and reputation gone.

The other Cock marched off in high galumph,
Flew on to a wall to be seen by all.
He was. For while he crowed in lusty triumph,
A hungry eagle heard and saw and swooped:
Carried him away for all his show.
The beaten bird came out from his retreat.
The matron hens and every pullet nymph
Made much of him. And he without compete
Made much of them in his seraglio.

42

THE KID AND THE WOLF

(Distance is the courage of the weak)

A kid, the son of a wealthy goat,
Small, spindly, soft as yolk,
Who lacked even the pluck to jostle
His brother for his mother's milk,
Saw from the top of a high roof
A grizzled wolf with hungry jowls
Loping towards his hunting grounds.

The kid, alert and safely proof
Against the other's thwarted walk,
Cocked his head with a forced laugh

And shouted: "Thief! Murderer! Wolf!
How do you have the nerve to prowl
In this bourgeois neighborhood
Of honest goats and pigs and fowl?
Wicked mammal! Criminal!"

The Wolf looked up with a vulpine smile,
Scathingly urbane, aloof.
"What a brave little thing!" he said.
"What courage from a high roof!"

THE WOLF AND THE HOUSE-DOG

(To be hungry and free is better than to be well-fed and a slave)

Master Wolf's lean and hungry looks
went to the heart of even Master Mastiff House-dog
as they exchanged glances in their tracks.
    "Down to skin and bone!" thought that one.
"It's the life he leads . . . no fixed meals,
no fire, no bed; no one to pay attention to his needs;
and precious little pickings—with us dogs watching out—
doesn't weigh a stone—I doubt."
    As these thoughts flashed through House-dog's glance,
Wolf was thinking this:
"What a sleek and portly swell!
I wonder what it's like to live so well?
Makes two of me. I dare not fight. Better be polite."
    As each thought his thoughts, and hesitated,
the House-dog with genuine concern
(though not without a smirk),
turned and said: "Cousin, like a bed?
Then why not work? You are too haggard.
I can set you up as my assistant.
The duties will be light,
the food first-class and the perks most generous.
Your improvement will be instant.
And no one need ever know that once you were a blackguard."
    The Wolf winced at this, but, hungry still, was staggered.
"Sounds all right," he said. "What do I do?"
    "Oh, just bark at people coming to the door.
It doesn't really matter who.
Shows you care,
even if half the day you're stretched out on the floor.
Be civil to the servants. Resist flying after Cook's cats.
Greet my Lord.
And when they pull you by the ear,

smile at my Lady's brats."

The Wolf agreed that these concessions would be slight
in return for bed and board.

Master Mastiff with a lordly lift of his head
when the mansion rose up into sight,
revealed too patently round his neck a balding white
circle where his collar chafed:

"What's that dull mark behind your ears?"
asked Master Wolf with sudden fears.

The House-dog turned and laughed:
"Nothing, my friend, nothing. Let me make that plain.
It's just the mark my collar makes at night."

"Your collar?" "Yes, the collar of my chain . . .
One soon gets used to it."

"Your chain?
Am I to understand you are not free to come and go?"

"Well, not exactly so . . . It's only a means to an end.
And who cares in such a good hotel?"

"Alas, _I_ do, my friend.
I'd rather do without your fire, fixed meals and bed.
All the chicken bones in Hellas
are of no avail to me—if I'm not free."

Saying which, he fled.

THE SNAKE AND THE CARPENTER'S FILE

(There is no sense in attacking the insensible)

A Snake of acidulous bile
Who assiduously flew at a file
    Could not help feel
    That biting at steel
Was futile after a while.

THE HERON WHO WAS HARD TO PLEASE

(Those who insist on perfection often end up with nothing)

A Heron early one morning stood in a stream
And fastened his eyes on every fish that passed.
"The dawn air gives me an appetite,"
He said to himself. "So I'll not waste my time
On the smaller fry. What I want is a large
Chub or a sleek fat trout."
Several elegant sizeable dace swam by,
Then a roach, but half an inch too small.
Finally a perch as big as a dish.
The Heron shook his head. "All bones," he said.
The sun climbed higher and the day advanced.
The fish now left the shallows for the pools.
But Heron stood there still unbreakfasted.
Hope, ambition, boredom kept him clamped
All day till sunset when a pigmy minnow
Came swimming by. This he seized and swallowed,
Gulping down his hunger with regrets.

THE LARKS AND THE FARMER

(If you mean business, see to it yourself)

Larks build their nests among the sprouting
Crops or in the young fields of grass,
In that season of the year when earth
Renews itself in festivals of love and birth.
This Lark was late, the hay was ripening,
She saw that she must choose a husband fast.

46

This she did: and laid, sat on, hatched
A twittering brood, with singular despatch.
But now the hay was almost fit for cutting.
"My dears," she said, "I'm off to find some food.
Keep your eyes open and your ears alert."
She returned to find the larklings in a panic.
"Mother, we heard the Farmer tell his son
He'd got his friends to promise they'd come at dawn
To cut our field," the nervous chorus cried.
"If that is all he said," the Lark replied,
"There's time enough. Enjoy your dinners. Grow."
At dawn the sun arose and climbed the sky,
But evidence of reapers there was none.
Two days later the Farmer came again
And the larklings heard him mutter to his son:
"The hay is ripe. Our friends have let us down.
I'll get our relatives to come at day break."
This time when the mother Lark returned,
She found her fledglings chittering with fright.
"Oh mother, all is up . . . his relatives,
And at daybreak . . . now we surely must . . ."
"Not a bit of it, my loves! You'll see.
Eat your suppers and let your bird brains rest."
And so it was: no sign at dawn of Farmer,
Son or relatives. But later on,
The young larks heard the farmer tell his son:
"What fools we've been. Tomorrow you and I
Shall take our scythes and together cut this hay.
If something's to be done, depend on no one.
Remember this until your dying day."
The Mother Lark, for once, appeared impressed.
"Now for the move," she said, and hustled every
Fluttering fledgling pell-mell from the nest.

THE TOWN MOUSE AND THE COUNTRY MOUSE

(Peace of mind and high living do not always go together)

"But my dear, how veritably charming!"
Smiled the Mouse from Town glancing down
With elegance and suave deceit on three
Dried-up peas and a dirty piece of crust.
"But I must confess the country air
And all this bucolic tranquility
Makes me want to rather sleep than eat."
She yawned and with an urbane nonchalance
Began to tell of how she lived in town:
Her comforts, style, her banquets every day.
"You don't say! ... Really! ... Every day?"
The Country Mouse with "oohs!" and "ahs!" and nose
Twitching—eyes like polished sesames—
Broke in at every turn, until at last
She must that very afternoon set out
With Town Mouse for the fleshpots of the town.
And that same evening over snowy linen
She ran amazed along the dining table:
Through streets of pasties, chicken, ham and jelly,
Down boulevards of silver lit by candle
And past ramparts made of solid pastry—
Oh my! and towers of bottled fire.
"You see, my dear, you see!" the Town Mouse said,
As whiskers waved electric with desire.
But hardly had the rural lass's teeth
Begun to undermine a tall croquette,
When her cousin shouted: "Quick, in here!"
And pushed her headlong in the nick of time
Behind the centre-piece, a jardiniere,
As on that very spot a maid set down
A platter opulent with roasted chine.
"Don't give it a thought," the Town Mouse said.

"Just be alert . . . Here, try this garlic bread."
"I might have been as flattened as a plaice,"
Ran the worry in the other's head:
"Death by weight and heat would not be nice."
Then from under the table, if you please,
A mastiff snarled and sauntered from the room.
"Honestly, my dear!" sniffed Country Mouse.
At last when all was quiet and cheese and ham
Began to beckon through the streets again,
The door burst open and the guests came in.
By then however Country Mouse had flown.
"I want no paté and no costly viand,"
She wrote by letter later from her quiet home:
"I'll keep to sweet frugality and peace of mind."

THE SAUCEPAN AND THE CHINA BOWL

(Relationships are never one sided)

A large and heavy Saucepan made of iron,
Together with a China Bowl, was left to lie on
The banks of a river, and when the tide arose
Floated off with her to where the river flows.
The China Bowl did all she could to keep
Far from the Saucepan—dared not even sleep;
Until the Saucepan uttered this reproof:
"Why shun me so, my friend, why be aloof?
You know I'd never bump against your sides."
The bowl keeping her distance still, replied:
"I'm sorry, sir, that isn't what decides.
I'm lost no matter which of us collides."

THE WOLF AND THE CRANE

(Don't expect just payment from a crook)

The Wolf's feast was spoilt by a splinter of bone.
It lodged in his throat and he coughed and hiccupped and poked
But could not get it away. "Great Zeus!" he thought,
"This can't go on. What am I going to do?
With my reputation, who in the world will help?"
Indeed, the animals fled from his path as he came.
However, he found at last a credulous bird,
A sedate and curious Crane with a beak as long
As the neck of a small giraffe. "Ah!" he thought,
"Just the bird for the job." And the bird agreed.
He said to the Wolf: "I'll try if you give me a fee."
"Of course, dear bird . . . whatever you want, or I'll die."
"Sit down," said the Crane. "Now stretch your neck up high . . .
No, higher . . . that's right. Now open your mouth."
"Aah," groaned the Wolf, with his mouth conspicuously wide.
"Don't talk," said the Crane. "It only closes your throat."
"N'aaah!" said the Wolf. "Keep still," said the Crane: "head up."
Then he deftly probed with his beak to the base of the throat.
"I feel it," he said—extremely deep." . . . "So do I,"
Gurgled the Wolf. "Keep still . . . Now I've got it,"
And the beak of the Crane gingerly lifted out
Of the wolfish throat a splinter the size of a pin.
The Wolf shook his head and licked his lips with a grin:
"What a relief!" "Now for my fee," said the Crane.
"Fee?" laughed the Wolf, baring his teeth to the gum.
"*You* inserted your head in the mouth of a wolf.
Your fee—don't you see—is to have taken it out again."

THE DOG AND THE WOLF

(Those who try to get too much out of a situation often end with nothing)

Dog was cornered. Wolf slavered. Wolf had every intention of eating Dog up.

His eyes blazed, his mouth twitched, his tongue dripped.

Dog, not daring to move, in fact frozen with terror, managed to drawl:

"Not now, Comrade. Don't you see how thin I am, and as dry as a clove? The meal would be premature, an irreparable error."

Wolf hesitated, and Dog went on:

"Listen, there's to be a wedding. Flutes and drums and banquets lasting for days. Come back at the end of it all if you really want to find me in bon-ton. You'll be amazed."

Wolf bristled and his pupils shone.

Present hunger fought with future greed.

"Oh yes," Dog went on:

"I'll be fat and juicy, oozing chicken, mayonnaise and garlic bread."

"Is that a promise?" Wolf said.

"Cross-my-canines! an absolute pact. Agreed?"

"Very well then, fatten up, stuff yourself. Five days from now you'll see me back. Till then you're freed."

In five days to the minute Wolf was at the barn door: haggard, delirious with hunger, his look dour.

"Where are you?" he howled.

"Up here."

Wolf looked up and saw Dog sitting on the roof out of reach: plump, in bel-point, opulently jowled.

"Come down at once, or I'll sue you for breach," he snarled.

Dog looked down with safe disdain.

"Not on your life!" he called. "You had your chance and failed. It won't occur again. You squeezed too hard."

THE COCK AND THE PEARL

(Worth is only relative)

A fine Cock, the pride of a certain barnyard,
Kicking up the litter among his court of hens,
Saw the clean gleam of something white.
"What ho!" he chortled, wagging his comb and eyeing
The object: "That's for me—or the one I favour."
All the hens dutifully watched him snatch
A round grain with the lustre of an ivory pea.
It was in fact a Pearl, dropped in the yard and lost.
The Cock weighed and balanced it in his beak
Then let it fall back into the litter. "Pearl,"
He said, "you may be a treasure to the world of men,
But a bushel of you in the realms of chickenhood
Has less value than a single barley grain."

THE BALD MAN

(The logic of natural ownership)

A Bald Man with a fine head of hair
 (Not his own but worn with a flair)
  Riding along on a highstepping mare
   Suddenly found in a puff of air
    His hair
    Not there.

When people guffawed at his distress,
 Reining his horse in, he said: "Yes,
  My coiffure's gone, but do confess:
   Didn't the man who grew it possess
    Even less
    Success?"

BELLING THE CAT

(A plan is useless if it cannot be carried out)

A single question was on the agenda: how to outwit the cat. The mouse conference dragged on. Finally, an up-and-coming mouse got to his feet and said:

"Comrade Mice, speaker after speaker has told us how his brother, his sister, his aunts, his mother, have fallen into the claws of the Cat. Very sad, but what is the point of these endless case histories? A cat-is-a-cat-is-a-cat and the slaughter will go on. We may be quick but she gets us in the end—simply by waiting. She is patient and her memory is long. We are impatient and ours is short. It is simple statistics."

54

The mice squeaked and nodded. Here was a young rodent who would go far.

"I have a plan," the mouse continued. "It is simple, radical and complete. It will solve our difficulty forever."

The room quivered with twitchings. Every whisker was charged.

"What we need is a system," he went on: "a system of alarms which is unfailing and ubiquitous. I mean," and he lowered his voice, "one that is automatically concomitant with the presence of the Cat."

Really, this young fellow was brilliant. The room chittered with admiration.

"All we have to do is to procure a bell: this to be dangled from the Cat's neck. Wherever she may be, wherever she may go, we shall be alerted to her slightest movement . . . As I said, the scheme is unfailing and ubiquitous."

The young mouse leaned back while he was cheered for several seconds. Then there was a slow rustle and an old distinguished mouse wavered to his hind legs.

"My colleagues," he said, "I congratulate our young friend on his ingenious plan. There is no doubt that it would be successful. A bell round the neck of the Cat would indeed mark her whereabouts at all times of the day and night. There remains, however, one trifling consideration. Which of us is to bell the Cat, and how is it to be done?"

THE GOAT AND THE ASS

(What you concoct for others may turn out to be your own ruin)

A Goat and an Ass in the same backyard
    lived much in each other's company:
The Ass honest but conspicuously backward,
    the Goat one of those appallingly envious persons
    who imagine everybody has something better than they.
This one turned her back on radishes, leeks and salsify
    (all easily filched from the kitchen gardens)
    simply because the Ass had hay.
Which would be like refusing brandy and black coffee
    just because somebody else was given café au lait.
Well, anyway,
    the Goat foraged about doing nothing till milking time,
    whereas the poor Ass trudged round a treadmill
    like a first-class donkey—all day.

"You great booby," said the Goat with thin-lipped derision
    and a caprine smile,
    as the Ass was taking a rest on a certain Sunday:
"What a dull life you lead: All work and no play.
Why don't you use some guile
    instead of trudging round the treadmill,
    throwing away
    the best years of your life . . .
Strikes me as little short of futile.
And soon you will be senile."

To which the Ass said—unsuspecting any wile—
    "Aye aye, I should like a holiday
    with time perhaps to wed
    a nice sleek wife . . .
But how do you use guile? What would you say?"

The Goat narrowed her envious eyes:
    "Just pretend to have a fit and fall into a pit,"
    she said. "That's the only way."
And she watched the simple Ass walk over to a hole
    and do his best to capsize
    himself into it.
He did not do it very well and he fell
    uttering a dismal bray:
    so seriously damaged by the drop
    that his lips began to froth;
    the doctor was summoned;
    the Ass's heart examined.

"What he needs is a genuine caprine broth,"
    said the doctor to the master,
"Right away:
    you know, a strong savoury concoction
    made out of a she-goat's liver.
Nothing, I assure you, will cure him faster."

So, the jealous, clever Goat—watching quite near—
    was given no option,
But seized, slaughtered and concocted to effect a cure
    that very same day.

THE FOX AND THE CROW

(Flatterers are not to be trusted)

Fox saw the Crow fly past
Heading briskly East-by-East:
In her beak a piece of cheese.
Immediately he was on the chase,
Panting through the fields he raced,
Arriving as she came to roost
A mile away as the crow flies
In a chestnut tree with branched floors.
Many stories down he called
Up at her as she still held
The cheesy morsel firmly billed:
"Madam, may I make so bold,
To tell you how the view from here
Moves me more than I can bear?
Your plumes, your sheen, your black, your beak
Make me want to hear you speak.
If heaven has given you as well
A voice to match, I swear I will
Be your slave through field and wood."
The Crow, flattered, opened wide
Her coarse mouth and crowed "Caw."
Fox caught the cheese with care.
"Thank you, m'dear, but can you afford
To trade mere flattery for food?"
Fox called up. "A costly lesson,
But well worth it if you can."

THE FOX IN THE OAK TREE

(If you wait, problems often solve themselves)

In the lean season a thin and hungry fox
Nosed his way and found beyond all hope
A cache of food which provident hands had stowed
Into the hollow enclaves of an oak.
The Fox fell upon it there and then,
Eating enormously, and then again,
Downing what was left after his nap;
Only to face a new undoubted fact:
That he had grown with his meal—waxed fat.
Now his stomach filled the narrow gap
And wiggle though he would, it did no good:
There he was as fast as in a trap.
"Oh my! Oh my!" he whimpered, "I am lost.
There's not a thing that I can do to oust
My swollen carcass from this blasted box."
A fellow fox who passed that way and heard
The gist of his defeated attitude,
Scoffed and said: "I think you're being absurd.
To very few is given such a deal:
To share a closet with so square a meal."
"Laugh if you want, but don't you see my state?"
The other barked, still panic-struck and bound:
"The meal may have been square but I am round."
"My friend, there is no problem: simply wait.
You've eaten all the food there is to eat. . . .
Contain yourself, relax, stay where you are.
Eventually you'll be just *as* you were."

THE CAT AND THE BANTAM COCK

(Nothing will stop a will bent on crime)

Mr. Cat,
   A hungry and a greedy beast,
   held in his claws a bantam Cock;
   and against all international law
   was determined to feast on him,
   but being a diplomat
   and hesitant to shock
   world opinion,
   he elected to delay the murder
   till he could conjure up a reason.
"You crow too loudly, sir, I say,"
and he gave the Cock a sinister squeeze.
"You wake men from their sleep—
   an unforgivable breach."
The Cock gasped out: "Please,
   this is only a way
   I make sure that mankind is awake."
"Well, there are things worse than that,"
   said Mr. Cat:
   "things I can hardly bring
   myself to utter."
"What, sir?"
   asked the Cock in a whisper
   so diffident it was not audible.
"Pervert! You stop at nothing . . .
   Sleep with your sisters,
   even with your mother?
   Incest . . . horrible!"
The Cock's comb blenched.
"But this, sir, too is only service,
   it provides more eggs for my masters."

Whereat the Cat,
    his eyes rapacious with green intent,
    held the Cock within an inch
    of a slavering face and spat:
    "That's hardly nice . . .
Meanwhile, all these specious pleas and special pleading
    are no reason I be kept from feeding."
And quite intransigent,
    he downed him in a trice.

THE TWO CRABS

(What we criticize in others is usually true of ourselves)

A mother Crab watching her Son with pride
and not without concern,
Said: "Son,
you're doing fine
but for God's sake learn
to walk straight ahead,
not obliquely, always to one side."

She spoke this scuttling sideways on her ragged claws.
The Young Crab watched her, then he said:
"Ready when you are, mother—right behind.
We can only go the way we are designed.
Show me how *you* manage floors,
For when it comes to progress
I must copy yours . . .
Or do you think me blind?"

THE GNAT AND THE BULL

(The self-importance of the petty person)

A Gnat who fondly thought herself a famous person
when really she was insignificant
and more than usually dull:
        (Only known
because of her inconsequent and gadding ways)
        One breezy afternoon,
        by way of a diversion,
        let herself be blown
onto the horns of a great and stalwart Bull,
and rested there ready to amaze.

        After several hours,
during which his lordship did not cease to graze
and plod among the grass and flowers,
        She tired of so little conversation
        (not to say of adulation)
and demanded him in an airy whine,
        which he could scarcely hear,
if he would rather that she went and he were left alone.

        "Madam," said the Bull,
"I had no inkling of your visitation.
Frankly, not to put too fine a point upon it, no idea
        that you were even here.
So, feel quite free to come and go, my dear."

THE LION IN LOVE

(Do not be meek beyond your nature)

A Lion of resplendent mane and fierce physique
Fell in love with a girl, a farmer's daughter.
And came to her parents roaring out his passion.
They, terrified but reluctant to surrender
Their darling, and too helpless and too antique
To risk enraging him, said: "Sire, you've sought her
In the full awesome prowess of your station.
We're delighted and we're proud. We'll send her
To you, but please remember she is weak
And the way of loving lions we've never taught her.
So will you, in devoted sublimation—
For fear your well-developed claws offend her—
Have them removed. And use a new technique
When you kiss her . . . we mean, that if you caught her
On your teeth it wouldn't be our fashion.
Please, then, have them pulled in case you rend her."
The loving Lion, deceived by such oblique
Tactics, trimmed his nails and toothless sought her.
But the crafty parents turned on him with passion,
No longer feared but mocked his ruined splendour.
They beat the defenceless beast and gave no quarter . . .
So are the strong reduced when they are meek.

THE MILKMAID AND THE SPILT MILK

(It is unwise to count your chickens before they are hatched)

The dairymaid Amanda stepped lightly through the fields, her milk pail balanced nicely on her head—it being the days when milkmaids balanced pails—and she hummed a positive, calculating kind of hum as she tripped along:

"The money from the milk'll buy a couple of laying hens... I'll get White Leghorns if I can—they lay the whitest, biggest eggs—not those greedy Rhode Island Reds, who'd guzzle through more money than I'd earn... Let me see, two eggs a day, seven days a week—no, not seven, can't expect the poor things to be absolutely clockwork—six then, means that in three weeks I can put down cash for that chintz frock dotted with bluebells just in time for the fair. My my, the young men are going to buzz around me! Won't Kitty Fisher be put out! The jealous, pouting thing! Serve her right. I'll snatch the fellows from under her stuck up nose. And I'll give her such a look. I'll just toss my head like this and ..."

Poor Amanda. She suited the action to the thought and gave her head the sauciest toss. Milk pail, milk and all came tumbling down. Woebegone and sadly empty headed, she reported home.

"Never count your chickens, m'am," her mother crossly said, "until you see them hatched."

THE FOX WHO LOST HIS TAIL

(Self-interest often lies behind advice)

A Fox—ace murderer of hens and geese—
Found that even a lifetime's expertise
Could not undo a single slip.
He walked into a trap,
And thinking he would die of shame
If his brother foxes found him there,
Managed to escape but left behind
The bushy glory of his tail.
"What shall I do?" he worried, slinking home.
"It's not merely the disfigurement
But loss of status that appals.
Everyone will guess what has befallen.
How shall I escape embarrassment?"
By and by, a gleam came to his eye.
He slipped into the wood and there
With his back against a tree,
Summoned all the foxes to a meet.
"See here, my brothers," he declared,
"I propose a new and stylish mode.
You may be shocked at first but soon you'll see
How right I am. For Nature was absurd
To burden us with tails and all their code.
Just think of them: the uselessness of tails!
They weigh us down just when we need to flee.
They catch in briars when the hounds give chase.
They sweep up mud from under rainy trees.
Off with them, I say. It is our duty.
Let us inaugurate a new and better day.
Let us advance towards enlightened beauty."
These observations, uttered with aplomb,
Drew from other foxes murmurs of esteem.
Several younger foxes hurried forward

Eager to be docked and lead the fashion,
Till one old fox dryly from his corner spoke:
"A proposal full of reason but, with your permission,
Will the speaker now oblige us by
Turning round a minute while we give it scope?"
His foxship turned, but could not turn the crisis.
A hurricane of laughter greeted his behind.
"You see," observed the sage cutting through the jokes,
"How, to gain a certain end,
Self-interest masks itself as good advice."

THE MIDDLEAGED MAN AND HIS TWO SWEETHEARTS

(Love attempts to reduce inequalities)

A certain businessman with a flair for the girls
Kept a couple in town unknown to each other.
One was much older than he was, the other much younger;
He himself being over his middle years
And just beginning to sprout a few grey hairs.
Each of the females adopted a feminine plan
Of bridging the gap between her age and her man's.
The older, ashamed of a lover much younger than she was,
Took every occasion to coddle his poll on her lap
Never failing to pluck from it all the hairs that were black.
The younger, desirous of making him younger than he was,
Never missed a chance to pillage his pate of the grey.
This alternation of skirmishes over his topknot,
(His head so assiduously mauled)
Soon settled for good his piliferous lot.
He stared at the mirror one morning appalled
To find himself neither black nor grey
But completely bald.

THE WOLF DRESSED AS SHEPHERD

(Deceit is usually discovered)

Wolf was worried.
His takings from the flock had dwindled.
Shepherd's new dog outsmarted him.
He felt swindled.
Then one afternoon, in the heat,
He slid out of the wood and saw
Both Shepherd and Dog asleep.
What was more,
The Shepherd's gear—
Hat, coat, pan-pipes and crook—
All lying on the grass quite near
In a neat heap.
"This is my chance," he thought.
"No more watching and waiting for *him*.
No more stray little lambs.
Now I can have the lot:
Abduct the whole flock,
Even the dams . . .
If a wolf can fox a man,
I can."
This he said, and put the hat on his head.
Next, on the brim
With some charcoal he wrote:
"I am Alfie the shepherd of these sheeps."
Then he donned the coat,
Put the pipes to his lips,
And blew out a long hesitant note.
It sounded false, as did his wolfish calls,
And far from attracting the flock
Awoke Shepherd and Dog.
The chase was on.

Wolf stumbled like an absurd dummy
In his long weeds.
Unable to fight or to run,
He tottered into a ditch by the edge of the woods.
They paraded him in public afterwards.
Even the "Sheeps" thought it was funny.

JUNO AND THE PEACOCK

(We cannot expect to have every gift)

The Peacock paraded before the goddess queen. He displayed his fan, his crest, the pavonine blue of his ruff: all gifts she had lavished on him. Then he glanced down at his toes and cleared his throat.

"Majesty," he said, "would you deign to improve my feet and my voice? I should like the feet of a gazelle and the voice of a nightingale."

The goddess looked at him: noted the hauteur of his walk and the demand in his voice, and decided he had gone far enough. When he repeated his request and added with an edge of importunity that after all he was her favourite bird, Juno swept the sky about her and just before she disappeared into the clouds, said over her shoulder with the iciest of smiles:

"Dear bird, you cannot expect to be first in everything."

THE DOG AND HIS OWN REFLECTION

(Greed loses the substance by grasping at the shadow)

The Dog hurried along with meat in his mouth,
The largest piece that he had ever been blessed with.
Already he savoured the juice where his molars pressed.
But, in the middle of the plank that crossed the stream,
He suddenly caught sight of himself in the water.
His heart thumped with a leap of greed and he halted.
"A piece of meat," he thought, "as large as this one,
And a dog no bigger than me. I'll snatch it from him."
Imagining which, he grabbed at his own reflection:
Opened his mouth and let the meat fall out.
It was carried away by the silently moving river.
He lost the real to grasp at a shadowy image.

THE MANY-FRIENDED HARE

(Friendliness is not the same as friendship)

The Hare thought of herself as a popular person.
"I know everyone," she said: "I never meet
Any animal but *I* pass on
A word or a smile. I think the world my mate."

Then one day she heard the bay of hounds.
The hunt was on. She ran and said to Horse:
"Quick, my friend, carry me to the dunes."
"Sorry, m'dear, I have to draw the hearse,"

"Much as I'd like to, Master's aunt is dead."
Hare ran off to Bull. "Oh please," she said,
"Just show yourself. They'd scatter if you did."
"Love to, but the breeders need my seed,"

Bull answered . . . "I think that Goat is free."
Goat was busy chewing on a thistle.
"You know I would, and take you to and fro,"
She said, "all you'd have to do is whistle.

My back, alas, is hardly strong enough
To carry you. I'm sure that Ram will help."
Hare ran to Ram: "Oh please, it is my life,"
She begged. "Or I'll be caught and chewed to pulp."

"I'm deeply sorry for you," Ram replied,
"But even sheep are not immune from dogs,
Try Calf. With cows they change their attitude."
Calf was busy at his mother's dugs

And almost cried when told the awful news,
"But you can see how young I am," he said.
By this time the hounds were hare-breath close
And Hare took to her own swift feet, pursued,

But fast enough to reach her cover safe.
There she lay exhausted while some wrens
Heard her utter this ironic laugh:
"Friendliness, I see, is not the same as friends."

THE BELLY AND THE MEMBERS

(The whole functions through its parts)

The Members of the Body are usually known
As the hands, the eyes, the ears, the lips, the nose,
The mouth, the neck, the feet, the legs, the brain . . .
But why go on at length? The point is this:
One day they all rebelled against their brother,
Lowly Belly. "Doesn't do a thing,"
They charged. "Flops around. Has no charm.
Just gets fatter while we work. The drone!
Well, we'll show him what he's worth and soon."

The Members of the Body went on strike.
Legs collapsed, refused to stand or stride;
Hands to fetch or hold and Mouth to feed.
Body waned through lack of nourishment.
Physique slumped into a lifeless heap.
Even Lips, which spoke so bold, were cracked
And in a desperate dried-up whisper croaked:
"Friends, the strike is off or we are dead.
Members, to your tasks. Get moving legs.
Ears, listen. Nose smell. Head
Use your brain again. Hands hold.
From now on, brothers, we must work together,
Or Body totters to its end of tether.
We may not know what lowly Belly does,
And think of him as greedy, soft and dull;
For all our members' sakes I say, however,
By heaven let him do that something well!"

THE REED AND THE OAK

(Survival sometimes lies in pliancy)

One might have thought the argument a foregone conclusion. Here was this fine up-standing Oak with his straight bole, burgeoning girth and already massive shoulders, and he said he was stronger than this other: this thin, weedy, effeminate Reed, who grew by the edge of the same pond.

Then came the famous storm. How differently they treated it! The Reed from the beginning watched it, played with its small rushes of breeze, wept and whined when the wind was struck with grief; swayed, veered, inclined, even bent double with docility when the gale rose up and raged.

And the Oak? From the first he stood rooted to his station, contemptuous of all that the elements could do. When the breeze stiffened, so did his branches. When the gale stomped through the skies, his leaves merely rustled. In the very eye of the storm his body scarcely creaked.

When the wind had consumed its cholic, and the last clouds had scudded into oblivion, the Reed stood anchored still to his post, pale perhaps from his whipping, quivering a little, but straight and delicate still.

But the Oak? It were better not to ask or look. Prone like one murdered, dragged from his own root-step: a picture of tragedy ... his splendid body ironically intact—hardly a branch broken—but deracinated, torn up, slain from his very stock, his life and future over.

THE FOX AND THE STORK

(We cannot complain if others treat us the way we treat them*)*

Fox invited Stork to dinner,
Too greedy and too mean, however,
To be a generous host, he planned
The meal only for his pleasure.
"You'll love the stew," he said, and ran,
Licking his chops, to table; slopped
The morsels into his gross maw,
Hardly glancing at his guest.
He'd put the portions into bowls—
Wide and shallow, one apiece.
Stork, sedate, walked to his place
And seeing his long and slender bill
Could make nothing of the meal,
Stood silent by and watched appalled.
"What—not like it?" queried Fox,
Who had already finished *his.*
"Too bad! But never mind, *I* do.
It won't be wasted. Not a bit."
And he nudged Stork out of the way.
Stork said simply: "Next time
I hope you'll come and honour *me.*"
"Delighted!" slobbered Fox half through
His second bowl.
              When next they met,
Fox arrived in excellent time
Avid for dinner. And Stork said:
"Welcome friend, you so love stew,
That's what we're having."
                  He led the way
To two tall jars with narrow necks
From which a fine aroma rose.
Fox, however, on his toes,

Could barely even get his nose
To the jar's lip, nor tongue to lick
The stew's brim, though he racked and stretched
Till his tongue almost left its sockets.
Aroma was what Fox got.
Stork went on with his agape,
Sucked up his stew with love and turned
Urbanely to his guest and said:
"What, no appetite? How sad!
I enjoyed myself so much
With you the other day, I thought
I'd repeat your recipe."

THE WOLF AND HIS EVENING SHADOW

(We can delude ourselves with our own conceits)

A Wolf who used to get high on
His Shadow at dusk, fought a lion,
   But soon found that length
   Did not reflect strength,
And that shadow was not made of iron.

THE CAT AND THE HENS

(Villainy can be detected by honest instinct)

A Cat of Satanic appetite
Whose visage froze small birds with fright,
Hearing that some Hens were sick
Seized a doctor's bag and stick
And rushed to proffer sham physic.
He thought he looked the very part,
Pretended even to a chart
For each beldame and pullet's case,
Enlarged his voice and slowed his pace,
Put on a slightly pompous grace.
But when he reached the chicken yard
He found the Hens' hostel was barred.
Furious at being forestalled
He stood outside and sweetly called:
"Dear Madame each and Mademoiselle
The doctor's come to make you well.
His bag is full of healing lotions,
Unguents, liniments and potions.
Let him in to sound your heart,
Feel your pulse and use his art."
The senior Hen with fruity voice
Said, "Sir, there is a better choice,
A surer balm, a faster cure:
Just remove yourself from here. '

THE PIG AND THE SHEEP

(There is something more personal than property)

A young pig who suffered no delusion
    as to the source
    of blackpuddings, bacon and ham,
    and of course pork,
    joined a flock of sheep
In the hope that if his life were ovine
    it would create the illusion
    he was one of them—
    in fact a lamb.
But in time,
    when he grew sleek and in his prime,
    the farmer singled him out,
    laid hands on him
And pulled him along by his snout.
"My fine fat friend,
    you are by no means in the right
    walk of life," he said:
"Your vocation is quite other . . . This must end."
When the Pig squealed and fought,
The other sheep rebuked him, saying: "Brother,
    why stir up such a bother?
We don't make such a fuss
    when he catches one of us."
    "That's all very well,"
Screamed back the Pig struggling free:
"When he lays hold of you he only wants your wool.
    In my case, don't you see,
    he wants *me*."

THE FOX AND THE MASK

(Emptiness can be masked by appearances)

A Fox in the attic had toyed
With the mask of a god; then annoyed,
    Said, "What if it's Zeus,
    I can't see the use
Of the look of a god if it's void."

THE CROW AND THE PITCHER

(What seems at first impossible can with thought be arranged)

The Crow stalked round the Pitcher, half-dead with thirst. She had already stretched her head over the top and peered into it. There was water in the Pitcher but so near the bottom that it was hopeless trying to get her beak to it. Then she pushed against the Pitcher, hoping to overturn it—for might she not be able to catch a trickle of water before it disappeared into the ground?—but the Pitcher was too heavy for her.

The sun blazed down and her thirst grew. She picked up a stone and thought: "If I hurl it hard enough, the Pitcher will break and at least I shall wet my beak. So she flew into the air, intending to drop the stone from a height, but her aim was not good and she missed. She was about to repeat the attempt, when another idea came to her: "What if I drop the stone gently inside the Pitcher, then another, then another—on and on? Won't the water at the bottom be forced to make room for the stones and gradually rise?"

This she proceeded to do, and legend has it that the water did indeed rise and that she was able to quench her thirst.

78

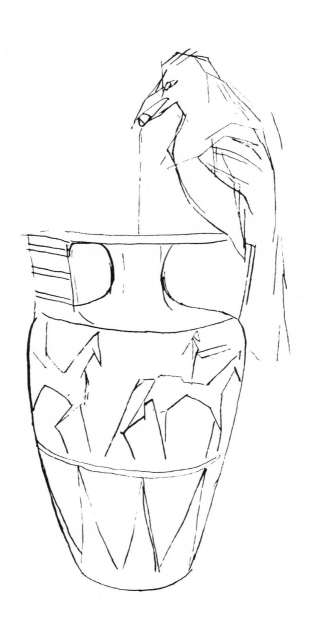

THE FOX AND THE GRAPES

(People will abuse what they cannot have)

A Fox who hour after hour
Had leapt at some grapes on a bower,
   Said: "Oh, go to Hades!
   I'd rather pick daisies.
Every grape here is seedy and sour."

THE FOX AND THE CICADA

(The intelligent learn from history)

   The Cicada sat
   In a tall pine.
   Her song was strong
   The sun hot,
   And she unseen.
   "She must indeed,"
   The Fox thought,
   "Be large and fat."
   "Madam, what tone!
   What volume, power
   You charge your song
   With! And how fresh!
   Madam, I long
   To see you near:
To see you in the flesh."

The Cicada did
Not stop her song
But dropped a twig
With a leaf attached,
And when she saw
The Fox attack,
Said, "Sorry, sir,
But you were wrong
If you really thought
I'd fall into your trap.

You see, my dear,
When I was young
One of the things
I early learnt
Was to suspect
A fox of plottings.
Yes, one of the things
I have to thank
Providence for
Is the day I saw
(If I may be frank)
Cicadas' wings
Shine in a fox's droppings."

THE HARE AND THE TORTOISE

(Steady application outdoes spasmodic brilliance)

"Hi!" said the Hare with a skip, "you slow old box . . .
Plod, plod—what a clip!—this hot afternoon.
I could race to the sun and back, I swear,
Before you started."

"I'm not very fast, to be sure," the Tortoise said,
"However, I carry my house upon my back,
I'm always there, and I'm not so slow as you think
Once I've started."

They challenged each other to race—Hare and Tortoise.
All the animals lined the course from wood to town.
The arrogant Hare gave a yawn and lay on the lawn,
So the Tortoise started.

Plod, plod, plod—he made slow progress
While the Hare on the lawn on the hot afternoon
Pretended to sleep to show how fast he was
Once he started.

Plod, plod, plodding—the Tortoise got there.
The Hare on the lawn fell asleep that hot afternoon.
He was roused by cheers. Oh, the Tortoise was there!
Poor Hare had not started.

THE HORSE AND THE ASS

(Selfishness can lead to a suffering self) .

The Horse
   danced along lightly:
   he had only his master on his back.
The Ass
   was loaded down with goods and chattels
   and the man's wife.
When he pleaded: "Horse,
   take some of my load, please:
   and you'll save my life,"
The Horse snorted this reply:
   "Beast, I am no hack.
   Our master has done quite rightly.
   I am a horse—you an ass."
It was not long before the Ass collapsed
   in the middle of the road,
   and died.
The man, of course,
   shifted his wife on to the Horse,
   together with all the Ass's packs—
   even the Ass's hide.
The Horse stumbled along.
Full of regrets and pain, he said:
   "Oh, I was wrong.
   If I had helped poor Ass
   I should never have come to such a pass."

THE ASS AND THE WOLF

(Only singlemindedness achieves its goal)

The Ass was too late to save her skin.
She knew that Wolf was almost on her.
She slackened her pace and began
to limp in a measured, quiet manner
as though she were hurt but resigned to her fate.
When Wolf came leaping up to her
she waited her cue.
"Master Wolf," she said with pathetic abandon:
"Let us be frank with one another. It is your nature
to eat me. *That* I accept. Though still young, my life is over.
But there is something that you ought to know:
something you never planned on."
When Wolf pressed her to be more explicit,
she hung her head.
"A minute ago I jumped over a hedge," she said,
"and landed on a large thorn."
Wolf said: "Oh . . . is it
still there?"
"Yes, it has lodged in my hind left hoof—
as hard as a corn. I advise you to pull it out so that when
you eat me it won't prick your tongue.
I thought I might save you a little pain . . . That is the truth."
Wolf thought this both considerate and sane.
He said: "I'm not a doctor but I'll do what I can.
Don't look so forlorn."
As he lifted up the Ass's hoof to examine it,
she summoned up all her strength and with perfect timing
delivered him such a kick in the mouth that it knocked out
all his teeth.
Wolf spluttered: "Charming!"
Stunned with shock and pain, he loped away
as Ass bounded off shouting: "Botcher!"

84

When he had got back his breath
he sat down and said to himself:

"She's right. I had no business meddling with medicine
when nature intended me for butcher."

THE BAT, THE BIRDS AND THE BEASTS

(One cannot be in two camps at once)

There was to be war between the Birds and the Beasts, and the Bat
thought to himself:

"How can I escape having to fight?" And he hung upside down
from the ceiling, thinking.

When the Birds sent a delegation to him, saying: "You are a
bird. You'll fight on our side, won't you?" He stayed where he was
and answered incredulously:

"How dare you ask! Don't you see I have fur and hang from
the ceiling?"

So the Birds flew away outraged and their place was taken by
a delegation of Beasts, who expressed to the Bat their certainty that
he would fight for them. This time the Bat flitted delicately from the
ceiling and squeaked in a highpitched unbeastlike voice:

"You must be mad. Don't you see that I fly?"

The Beasts lodged this remark in their hearts and went away.
Soon afterwards the Birds and the Beasts resolved their differences.
There was no war, but universal gladness. In the midst of which
the Bat flew among the feasters saying that he was overjoyed and
could he as both bird and beast join the celebrations?

"Not on your life," they replied. "You belong to none of us.
Off with you before we maul you to pulp or peck you to pieces."

THE DOG IN THE MANGER

*(There are persons who, when they can't have what they want, make
sure that no one else can)*

The manger was heaped with fresh hay.
    It was the siesta hour.
So Dog climbed, curled up and lay
    in the kernel of this bower.
Horse who worked in the fields all day
    came home and thought he would devour
A little of what he fancied did him good;
    only to find Dog, well-rested,
Sitting on top of his food.
    "I'm glad my manger's been of use,"
He said as nicely as he could:
    "Now do you mind leaving so that I can feed?"
Here Dog began to hurl abuse.
    Even though hay if ingested
Could hardly be—by Zeus!—
    a fodder he digested,
Dog wanted everything for *him.*
    And now when Horse approached he acted grim:
Snarled, barked, bit and tried to maim.
    "Alas," said Horse walking away, "your game
Is played by every envious man and woman when
    they can't have what they want,
So see that no one can."

THE GNAT AND THE LION

(Victory over the greater does not guarantee victory over the less)

The hybristic Gnat
Knew exactly what she was at
When she attacked.
Circling round the Lion's head
She trumpeted:
"I'm not afraid of you,
Great brute!
You're the least of my foes.
What can you do
With your teeth and your claws,
Still less with your roars?"
Proclaiming which, she flew
Straight for the Lion's nose,
Planted her sting,
And then on the wing
As Lion tossed and fumed
She whined and hymned
Her needling melancholic tune,
Then, flying jubilant ahead,
Flew into a spider's web.
And as the spider bound her
(Wings and feet)
For a coming feast,
The Lion heard her sound her
Penultimate lament:
"O victorious Gnat!
O irony of fate!
O conqueror of cats!
What did you think you were at?
And now you learn too late."

THE HORSE, THE STAG AND THE HUNTER

(If you use others you must expect them to use you)

The Horse and the Stag ran free vying with each other for supremacy, until one day the Horse had the brilliant idea of enlisting on his side the prowess and sagacity of Man. So he accosted a Hunter and asked:

"Will you help me against that upstart Stag?"

The Hunter, tired of hunting on foot, quickly replied:

"Certainly, come to my hut."

When the Horse stood outside the man's hut, pawing the ground, the Hunter said.

"You must do as I say ... Put this piece of iron between your teeth and this halter over your head and let these reins be attached to both—all so that I can guide you. Good. Now submit to this saddle on your back so that I can sit on it and direct you swiftly towards the foe."

The Horse complied with these requests and soon the pair of them, Hunter and Horse, proved too strong for the Stag and overcame him. Then said the Horse:

"I am grateful to you, sir. I could not have done it alone. Now will you please get off my back and remove these trappings."

"Wait a minute," retorted the Hunter. "This relationship between you and me suits me well. I have you under bit and bridle and I prefer to keep you that way."

THE EMULATING KITES

(Keep to your own talents)

It is said that the kite
    (a bird which is something between
An eagle and a hawk),
    Once could sing
As well as any swan.
    It is further said that the kite
By trying to copy an alien tune
    lost his own.

The Kites were circling over a field
    and they heard from the heights,
From mare, stallion and frolicking fold,
    a fresh wild sound that went right to their hearts:
Neighing, whinnying and what they thought
    were musical snorts.
Immediately, all the Kites in the air were set
    on copying this sound they had not got.
The breeze on which they balanced was rife
    with every kind of squeak and sneeze,
In the vain endeavour to bring off
    the noise they could not realize.

Never was heard for weeks
    their own beautiful song,
Until one day an elder of the Kites
    at a conference on the wing
Said: "Stop, my chicks, something's terribly wrong.
    All we do is caterwaul like cats.
In our efforts to learn something new
    we have not learnt to neigh
And have forgotten how to sing."

THE MAN, THE BOY AND THE DONKEY

(Try to please all and you will please none)

"Let's not sit on him," the Man said,
    "we want him to be fresh when we arrive."
"I see," said the Boy, "we'll get a better price
    if he looks alive."
They were taking their Donkey to market,
    all three of them walking along.
"You're crazy!" shouted a passing farmer.
    "What's a donkey for if not to ride?
    That's if he's strong.
If not, and you sell him—that's wrong."
So Man put Boy on Donkey, feeling he had done right.
But when they passed a group of workmen mending
    a signpost that had blown down in the night,
They heard one say: "Just look at that boy
    sitting up there like a rajah while
    his poor father walks—what a sight!"
The Man turned to his son. "Get down," he said.
    "We'd better change our roles."
This they did and it seemed a good solution
    till they passed two women gossiping,
Who with sour faces said: "Look at that great oaf!
    Leaves his little boy to do the walking!"
So Man took son up next to him and all was well until
    on the outskirts of the town
    they saw people pointing at them, talking.
Someone shouted: "Fancy those two obese hulks
    sitting on the overloaded beast!
    How can they do it?"
    This made Man go red.
"We must get off, son. Oh, I knew it!"
"We've tried every blessed combination," Boy replied,
    "except carry the beast ourselves."

90

"You're right," Man said:
"If we string him to a pole there's nothing to it."
So they cut a pole, strung Donkey up
    and carried him head down.
When the people saw this odd procession,
    they cheered and laughed running out of town.
Meanwhile Donkey was not happy.
His ankles were red, the blood rushed to his head,
    and his ears were floppy.
In the middle of the bridge Boy stumbled,
Man cursed, Donkey kicked, knots snapped, pole broke,
The whole rolled over the edge into the river.
    Donkey went down like a stone.
Man and Boy could only look over the ledge and shiver.
Then an old peasant who had watched the thing from the first
    said: "That was not very clever.
If you take advice from everyone,
    you'll never do anything—ever."

THE MOUNTAIN AND THE MOUSE

(There are people who after spectacular exertions produce little)

The village at the foot of the Mountain rocked, the earth rang. Everybody stood in the square gazing upwards as smoke and a hail of boulders poured from the Mountain into the sky. Trees were uprooted, the river changed its course. Everyone waited. The crashing and roar of the Mountain grew. Still they waited. Then suddenly one side of the Mountain split and everything stopped. In total silence there emerged out of the abyss—A Mouse.

THE LION, THE WILD ASS AND THE FOX

(The intelligent are guided by circumstance)

"We shall make an association of three, a profitable triumvirate," said the Lion: "my strength, Master Ass's speed, and Master Fox's cleverness. . . . Come, ahunting we will go."

The chase was all that the Lion had hoped. The game were tricked by the Fox, caught by the Ass, and finished off by the Lion. The bag was considerable.

"Divide it up, will you," said the Lion to the Ass grandly. So the Ass divided up the spoils into three scrupulously equal parts, and reported to the Lion.

"The division is made, sir. Choose whichever of the three you fancy. I assure you, they are all the same."

A look of fury came into the Lion's eyes, and with one swipe of his giant paw he felled the Ass where he stood and left him lying next to the three heaps he had made. Then the Lion turned to the Fox.

"See to the proper division," he said with a majestic yawn.

"At once, sire," the Fox returned, and in a quarter of the time it had taken the Ass to assemble the booty, the Fox made two piles. One contained almost everything; the other, a few paltry trifles.

"Majesty, choose whichever appeals to you," he said to the Lion.

The Lion walked over to the larger pile and said, "How just and fair you are! Who taught you to divide so correctly?"

"*He* did," answered the Fox, pointing to the dead body of the Ass.

THE TWO RIVERS AND THE SEA

(Some people illogically blame others for their condition)

Two rivers complained that the Sea
Changed them from fresh to salty.
   Said the Sea: "If the brine
   Is not in your line,
Then why do you flow into *me*?"

THE WIND AND THE SUN

(Gentleness can do what violence cannot)

The month was April: time when sun and wind
Vie with one another for their roles.
As usual, they were arguing. "I'll tell
You what," said Sun, retiring behind a cloud:
"See that man coming down the road?
He's got his greatcoat on. If you can have
It off him in five minutes, then I'll bow
To you, concede you have more power than I."

"Right!" said Wind, "I'm beginning now . . .
Ha, hoo, hi, blow, heave!
Swish, puff, buffet, whiffle, shove!
He doesn't know what's hit him. Golly, whoosh!"
Wind's cheeks were fat just like a cherub's
Bursting breath across an ancient map.

He soughed, roared, growled, yelled, whined;
Sent tiles prancing, leaves dancing, blew
Lampposts down, papers up, clouds
Scudding—all for the sake of one greatcoat.
But far from loosening it, this pandemonium
Only made the victim turn his collar up
And button every button that there was.
In vain did Wind flap, belly, squall.
The man wrapped himself as tight as a cocoon.
"That'll do," said Sun, beaming from a cloud.
"You've had your turn—and what a turn—watch *me*."
Whereat he shone upon the man in glory,
Warmed the air, stilled the trees, lit up
The countryside until the man felt something
Like a smile stealing through his blood.

In two minutes he had thrown his collar open;
In three undone his buttons, and before
Five were over, tossed his coat off, slung
It with a look of cheer upon his arm.
"You see," laughed Sun, "you cannot doubt I won.
Gentleness can do what tantrums can't."

THE FOX AND THE ASS IN THE LION'S SKIN (i)

(He who proves too much disproves all)

Said a Fox to an Ass in a Lion's skin
    Who insisted on imagining
        That by this touch
        He had a lion's clutch
        And was really such
    And could frighten everything:
        "My friend, you bray . . .
        And well you may:
        You prove too much."

THE FOX AND THE ASS IN THE LION'S SKIN (ii)

(Frauds overreach themselves)

        An Ass in the Skin of a Lion
        (Which he'd filched from a tree
    Where some hunters had left it to dry on)
        Ee-awed and brayed:
        "Let all be afraid
        Of me: don't you see,
With my jaws and my claws and my terrible roars
    I'm a lion—I'm a lion—I'm a lion?"
        Which was all very well
        Till down in the dell
    A Fox who'd been keeping his eye on
        The total charade
        Jeered: "Shucks! who's afraid?

96

Naturally no one. For why on
Earth should your paws and your claws
And your terrible roars
(When not in fact yours)
Be anything you can rely on?
Your assinine bray
Just gives you away.
This may be all right for a try on,
A try on—a try on—
But you're not my idea of a lion."

THE STAG AND HIS ANTLERS

(Our best parts are not always those we think)

A young Stag, seeing his image in a stream, lifted his head with a spasm of joy:

"How beautifully my antlers grow! Who would not be proud of such personal and branched distinction?"

Then looking down he caught sight of his feet, and shuddered.

"What spindle shanks! What bony knees—the sublime to the ridiculous ... If only I had antlers on my under half as well!"

That same day the hunters came, and he bounded through the forest as they pursued. All would have been well—he was faster than the fleetest horse or hound—but as he tore through a thicket his antlers caught in a hazel copse. There he struggled, but the hunt was soon upon him and he found himself surrounded. As the dogs leapt forward an arrow pierced him. Then in his heart he cried out these words, his epitaph:

"O foolish Stag! Your horns went to your head.
With your feet alone, you would not now be dead."

THE LIONESS AND THE VIXEN

(It is quality not quantity that matters)

A Lioness mocked by a Vixen
For whelping a litter of one,
   When the Vixen had nine,
   Said; "Ah, but then mine
Although only one is a lion."

THE FOX AND THE ASS'S BRAINS

(Wit is always at the ready)

Yes, this Fox was resourceful, witty, and a great persuader.
First of all he persuaded the King himself, the Lion,
To go on a hunt with him, knowing full well that even
Without the "Lion's share" his bag at the chase would be weighty.
Then he persuaded the Lion to invite the local Ass
To his house, aware that the beast would be flattered enough to come.
Which is just what happened. The moment the Ass was inducted,
The Lion—at a wink from the Fox—sprang and brought him down.
"Dinner for today," the Lion declared. "But paws and teeth off,
I say . . . until this evening. Now for my siesta."
So the Lion lay down and the Fox watched till he heard him
    snoring.
He circled the savoury Ass, then with a deft incision
Cleanly extracted its brains and silently ate the morsel.
When the Lion woke up and went to the Ass for his dinner,
He found his favourite hors d'oeuvre—the delicate brains—was
    missing.

He turned on the Fox with a roar, in a terrible voice demanding:
"What have you done with the brains? I told you to leave him
    alone."
"Brains, Your Majesty? Brains? This ridiculous Ass had none.
He swallowed your invitation, didn't he, to dine?
How else could he have been so completely assinine?"

THE SOW AND THE BITCH

(Disputes about excellence are all relative)

Two proud mothers were disputing, a Sow and a Bitch. They lay
in opposite corners of a barn abusing one another, their brood all
around them.

"A 'litter' is the right word for it," snorted Sow, cushioned in
her amplitude and heaving between each word. "*Mine* is a 'farrow'."

"So what?" returned Bitch, bristling a little and nosing a particu-
larly greedy pup off one of her teats. "*I* bring my litter into the
world with the greatest of ease, but you puff and blow over your
farrow. 'Soughing' is it?"

"No more than 'bitching'... Anyway, so would you if they
weren't such miserable little bits of gristle and marrow."

There was silence while Bitch thought of what to say.

Sow continued to heave and to sigh, Bitch to bristle and nuz-
zle, and the young of both to suck.

"My litter has ten to it," said Bitch. "Your farrow has only
eight."

"Quite right, but my eight all have eyes. Your ten are blind."

And so the two mothers continued to score off one another and
their children to gorge and to grow... establishing nothing but that
the ego is proud of whatever it is, and that both excellence and
inferiority are relative.

THE FOX AND THE BRIAR BUSH

(There are people who run for help to the very ones who would destroy them)

The Fox in the Briar Bush crawled
Out of it bleeding. Appalled
   By his scratches, he cried:
   "I did not decide
To fall off a wall to be mauled."

"I think you are foolish to scold,"
Said the Briar, "and foolishly bold
   To fall into me
   When could you not see
It's my nature to grab and to hold?"

THE JACKDAW IN BORROWED PLUMES

(Most ludicrous is the uncovering of cheats)

A Jackdaw of satiric eye
With no more conscience when he lied
Than a wagonful of monkeys, once
Said to himself without a blush:
"Almighty Zeus has told the birds
That since there is a king on earth
He'll crown a king of air as well,
And who so fitted as myself?
The choice does not depend on wealth
But breeding, finery and beauty,
And who can look the greatest swell."

100

Then seeing his image in the river
(Where other birds were grooming figures,
Prinking for the coming contest),
He was appalled he looked so modest:
Not even proper raven black
But dullest kind of charcoal matt.
So going the round among his colleagues—
Peacocks, parrots, finches, eagles,
Pink flamingoes, virgin seagulls—
He watched and deftly filched from them
(Wherever they had shed a feather)
Whatever he could fit on *him*;
And in the end looked so arresting
That Zeus upon a prankish whim
(And really thinking him grotesque),
Of all the birds pronounced him best.
But just before he crowned him king
The others recognised their things.
"That's mine," a peacock cried,
Snatching back an argos eye.
"And so is that," a parrot spat,
"That's my collar, give it back."
Then an outraged cock, perplexed,
Said, "Look, the fellow's got my neck!
Those little feathers are my sheen."
The birds of the air all shrieking "cheat!"
Fell upon him with their beaks
And when they'd plucked him to the skin
Asked Zeus if he was still their king.

THE ANT AND THE GRASSHOPPER

(In the days of plenty we must prepare for the days of need)

"What industry!" said the Grasshopper as she watched the Ant drag an enormous sunflower seed over hill and dale. "Today it is sunflower seeds, yesterday it was grains of barley, and before that grass-seed . . . and the weather is so fine and warm . . . What will it be tomorrow?"

"Tomorrow it will be winter," said the Ant grimly, "and I advise you to lay in stocks."

"But my motto is 'Live in the present,'" answered the grasshopper brightly. "Besides, there is such abundance all around us it is ridiculous to toil and moil all summer long."

Saying which, she hopped on to a tuft of grass, swivelled her long body to face the sun, and trilled out a series of joyous notes as brittle as hay.

Some months later the picture was different. The leaves had fallen from the trees, the wheat been cut, and the first frosts had decimated the late flowers. A bedraggled and shivering Grasshopper made her way stiffly to the Ant's nest.

"Sister Ant, have pity on me," She called. "I know you have stocks of grain and seed for distribution to the needy. I am starving."

"They are for distribution to those who laid them in," returned the Ant from the bowels of her warm home. "I seem to remember that you were not one of them."

"No, but I sang," said the Grasshopper, with the pathetic trace of a chirrup. "Yes, all summer long I sang."

"In that case," came the curt reply, "all the winter you can dance."

THE STORK AND THE DYING SWAN

(Why should death be feared?)

A Stork being present at the song
        of a dying Swan,
Said: "Madam, tell me is there reason
        for song so out of season?"
To which the Dying Swan inclined
        her head and spoke her mind:

    "I enter now
        into that estate
    Wherein no more
        shall I be taken
    By gun or snare
        or fox, nor in the thrall
    Of winter hunger.
        Who would not rejoice
    At such deliverance,
        where death is but farewell
    And peace is all?"